The PM Leader Handbook
Leading and Managing Projects

~ One Team, One Mission ~

Ed Daniel

Copyright © 2012 by Ed Daniel

The PM Leader Handbook

ISBN-13: 978-1480087361

ISBN-10: 148008736X

First Edition

All Rights Reserved

Printed in the USA

The PM Leader Handbook

Dedicated to Defenders of

Liberty,

Past, Present and Future

October 2012

Ed Daniel

Introduction

~ In the complex world of teamwork, simpler is better. ~

There is leading and there is managing. In any mission-oriented endeavor both skill sets are required for the effort to achieve full potential or even succeed at all.

A person can become a good manager by getting organized and teaching others around him to follow processes and do work consistently. But becoming a good leader involves knowing and living core principles and inspiring them in others, all in the name of achieving common goals and not just grinding out daily work.

Leadership skills blended with management skills on targeted initiatives…this is where Project Manager Leaders come in. And that's the focus of this field-tested handbook, a distillation of practical approaches, techniques and principles that together drive consistent success on any type or size of project mission.

The PM Leader Handbook

Contents

This handbook is organized in mutually supporting sections:

Page 1 - **Planks**: basics of forming and leading a team on a mission

Page 11 - **Principles**: practical & philosophical rules leaders follow

Page 19 - **Skills**: skills needed to effectively manage and lead

Page 61 – **Conclusion**: *The PM Leader Handbook* in context

■■

Appendices

Page 63 - **A: Common PM Leader Pitfalls**

Page 65 - **B: PM Training; Role-Play Scenarios**

■■

Page 67 - **About the Author**

Page 69 - **About the Logo**

Ed Daniel

The PM Leader Handbook

Planks

Planks are the basic steps required to plan and lead a mission.

Ed Daniel

Planks

Planks are the fundamental "how-to" steps used by the leader to achieve success in a common cause. In the case of Project Management I've found they are: **Know the Mission**, **Know the Team**, **Know the Plan**, and **Lead the way**.

Know the Mission

The PM must know the project's mission and intent in order to devise a plan and achieve the desired outcome. A project sponsor defines project mission and intent. PMs ensure the intent is fully understood and explicitly accepted by all concerned. The PM will seek guidance and "barrier-to-progress-removal" assistance from the sponsor, who is senior enough, and wields enough organizational power, to see that project needs are met. The PM reports to the sponsor. Having a senior project sponsor, or "champion," is critical to the success of a project; the PM should not proceed without one.

**Quick Ref **

1. Know the Mission
- Define the intent/end state
- Establish mission champion
- Establish barrier removal process*

* Process by which a project sponsor is made aware of significant barriers to project success and then works to remove the barriers. Typical "barriers" are resourcing and/or are scope-oriented but can be anything impeding progress that the PM cannot resolve on his own.

Know the Team

The project team can be resourced a number of ways. Sometimes the team is explicitly assigned, sometimes the PM must corral the resources from approved pools, and sometimes the PM works with sponsors to request resources. Regardless, it's ultimately the PM's responsibility to secure the right tools for the job.

Once the team is identified, the PM starts the process of getting to know them. There are many techniques for doing this – "ice breakers," team building exercises, social outings, etc. As the team starts to get to know one another, the PM will conduct sessions to establish team "norms." Some examples of team norms are: team work location and hours expectations, roles and responsibilities, meeting cadence and styles, issue escalation procedures, time reporting procedures, standard project tools and document management procedures. For IT projects there will also be project format considerations like "Agile" vs. "Waterfall" and project management software tool variations (e.g. MS Project (MSP) vs. a Clarity portal, requirements management tools, test management tools, etc.).

As the team spends time together, the PM develops a feel for members' strengths and weaknesses. He needs to know the capabilities and personality of each teammate and develop the appropriate level of professional trust and confidence based on factors like past and current performance, reputation, and the PM's own judgment and observations. The team will also strive to know and eventually trust the leader in return. The PM should be himself and strive to be as clear, concise and open as possible in working with the new teammates.

Quick Ref

2. Know the Team
- Get the right skills for the mission
- Set roles & responsibilities expectations
- Get to know the teammates
- Let them get to know you
- Be clear, concise and consistent

Know the Plan

The PM will work with the team to create the project plan. It is the team's plan but the PM is responsible for its successful execution. The plan can have many facets and be documented many ways. But at its core the Plan/Schedule is essentially a listing - usually a spreadsheet or MSP plan - of interdependent work steps and milestones, with all tasks assigned and owned by individuals who commit to completing them by negotiated due dates.

But that isn't all it is. In fact, the format of the plan is much less significant than the PM's command of it, his ability to get and keep the team solidly behind it, and his ability to work with the sponsor and customer to control scope, schedule and cost appropriately. There are many factors affecting how the plan is created and managed, but one factor is consistent: *the PM is expected to know the status of the plan's execution at all times.*

On larger and more complex projects PMs must delegate task accomplishment to team leaders and performers, who ensure detailed work is progressing as planned and keep the PM informed of "work stream" status.

The relationship between the PM and work unit managers, team leaders, and individual performers will test the PM's leadership skills. This is because of the great need for mutually earned trust and commitment among team members, as well as between the PM and project sponsor. Generally speaking this trust must be built through reliable and competent performance over time. Serious breaches of trust, commitment, confidence, or judgment can be extremely detrimental or even fatal to the project effort and mission accomplishment.

Quick Ref

3. Know the Plan
- Build/maintain a simple flexible plan
- Involve the team in planning; it is the team's plan
- Ensure commitment from all parties to the project mission
- Expect and demand good judgment from management personnel
- Develop trust and confidence between team members and the leader

Lead the Way

The PM leads the team in staying on target from initial planning through successful project completion.

Tweaks to task and milestone target dates will be necessary, and there will be downstream effects of such changes. The PM creates and maintains the schedule, and is well positioned to make minor trade-offs and negotiations with performers. He also addresses significant changes in schedule, cost and scope with the project sponsor such that all parties remain aware of project status.

A normal status-reporting cadence tends to be weekly, but can be as often as daily or as infrequent as monthly or quarterly. Since bad news can never wait, a key PM role is to identify and report significant issues, changes, or obstacles to stakeholders as soon as possible. Unaddressed issues at lower levels can create fear, disruption and confusion for project performers, especially if not handled effectively by the PM.

The PM is prepared to take responsibility for his team as he works with the project sponsor to make fixes and remove obstacles. The PM must also be prepared to recommend personnel changes should they become necessary. In short, the PM is expected to lead the way.

**Quick Ref **

4. Lead the Way
- Work the plan
- Remove obstacles
- Communicate clearly

Ed Daniel

The PM Leader Handbook

Principles

PM Leaders use principles as guideposts in decision-making.

Principles

PM Leaders manage schedules, processes, and procedures. They also lead people and teams. In both roles the effective leader stays aligned with key principles. These guideposts support PM decision-making and personal interactions with teammates and sponsor(s). The more the PM follows these principles consistently, the more respect he will command and the more likely the project is to succeed.

Simplicity
By definition projects tend to be complex. Bringing an interdisciplinary team together on an ad-hoc basis to perform is inherently difficult. Many projects are just that, teams pulled together with little to no experience as a unit, being led by someone they've never met before. So give the project its greatest chance for success by keeping things as simple and clear as possible.

Integrity
Teams that can't count on colleagues and leaders to deliver as promised don't do well. Act with integrity and strength of

character and expect the same of your team and sponsor.

Judgment
The team and sponsor are counting on the PM. In order to lead effectively he must problem-solve. Successful problem solving requires assessing causes and applying good judgment in identifying and implementing solutions. Leaders may not have the expertise to solve the details of every problem, but they are expected to rely on others and make subtle judgments about whom to trust and to what extent. The leader must know when, where and to whom to raise the red flag signaling the need for help. Judgment will improve with experience as mistakes are made and lessons learned. Good PM Leaders learn from the mistakes of others as well as their own. They tend not to make the same mistakes twice.

Finally, sooner or later PMs will be witness (and victim) to errors in judgment on the part of the sponsor and non-project team managers. One of the most difficult aspects of PM leadership is successfully dealing with such lapses in judgment, since often the PM is powerless to solve the issues and can only act as an "influencer." In this role the leader tries to both mitigate effects on team members and work with offending parties to make corrections.

Openness
A leader should be approachable so the team can keep him informed and seek counsel regularly and painlessly. This keeps team members from wasting time dealing with issues that are best solved by the PM, and allows them to focus on their work. Leaders can and do have many personality types – all can be successful. But a leader who is not open and accessible severely limits his potential for success.

Honesty
Complex endeavors require a high degree of honesty. Problems come up. They need to be resolved quickly. Without a high degree of intellectual honesty and habitual forthrightness on the part of the team, this process is greatly hampered. Lack of honesty can manifest in people problems, process problems, and technical problems. All can be massively short-circuited with insistence on a high degree of honesty in the project team environment. The leader sets a tone of frank openness through personal example and explicit expectation setting.

Trust
When people work together towards a common goal the load is shared. Teammates must trust each other to shoulder respective loads. Trust is a precious commodity. It is dearly earned and when lost, only painfully restored. Team members need to be able to trust their leaders implicitly. Don't let them down.

Competency
The team is absolutely counting on the PM. So leaders must know what they are doing. In the event you don't know exactly what to do, seek guidance or pick the best option. Have a mentor and get smart quickly. Work very hard at this and readily admit when you are wrong. If the leader does so, the team will know it's okay to make honest mistakes. Promote the culture of 100% effort but not a zero defects mentality. Fix mistakes quickly, learn the lessons and move on.

Consistency
The PM Leader must be consistent in his behavior and attitude. Everyone has bad days, but PMs be cautious not to let personal problems darken your mood with

the team. The leader needs to be a positive influence in order to be effective and promote good team and individual morale. He sets this example consistently.

Loyalty
If your team bonds in a healthy way, you will have achieved a degree of mutual loyalty, to each other, to the team and to the mission. This is key and can serve to hold the team together when nothing else will. Loyalty works in all directions and is earned across the project team construct. Leaders stick up for their people. Ideally teams are held to high standards and have earned the leader's loyalty.

Commitment
Commitment comes with loyalty and trust. The PM Leader will initially be granted a degree of trust, loyalty and commitment by the team. After that, the leader's competency, consistency and commitment will determine the team's continued willingness to follow and perform. Be competent. Be committed.

Reliability
The leader must be reliable. The team is counting on this. When you've earned the

team's trust, they will weather the unplanned surprises common to projects. The expert project team performs as well on the contingency path as on the planned path.

Courage
It's not easy being the leader. PMs hold teams accountable as individuals and collectively. Inspire them to perform. Admit when you are wrong, and fight for the team when necessary. Don't shrink from difficult, time-sensitive decisions for lack of perfect information. It takes an extra measure of courage to be the leader.

Compassion
Feel and show compassion as the leader. Expect excellence and accountability. Team members are accountable but not perfect. A little compassion and empathy for mistakes can go a long way. A strong team is an extended family and takes care of one another. Demonstrating compassion starts with the leader.

Be yourself
Leaders have all manner of personality types. Your team will see who you really are. If you haven't already done so, take a

personality inventory like the Myers-Briggs or Personalysis. Discover the facets of your personality as others see you. Polish your rough edges. Accentuate your strengths. Know yourself. Be yourself.

The PM Leader Handbook

Skills

PM Leaders use key skills to lead and manage effectively.

Ed Daniel

PM Skills

Let's look at specific skills the leader will need to employ:

Interpersonal Communications

Complex team endeavors require clear, effective communications. The PM Leader is at the heart of these communications.

In a workplace environment where email, texting, telephone, blogging, and old-fashioned face-to-face meetings are all options, the leader must first decide on the mode of communications. Many factors affect this decision, including: the sensitivity and nature of the communication content, the personal relationship between the parties, time of day/day of the week, time zone differences, etc. Examples of good mode choice include: choosing to postpone a difficult conversation until it can be conducted in person, or, choosing to send an email instead of a text when a little more formality is in order. The wrong mode choice can doom the communication from the start.

Listening is another key interpersonal

communication skill. That is, listen first to understand the situation and speaker's message. This way the speaker gets the opportunity to be heard first and will more likely be cooperative. The leader gets the benefit of responding with more complete information.

Timeliness is also important. Communications often lose some or all of their value if not delivered in a timely fashion.

Remember to tell the truth. Using tact is great, and can help soften difficult messages. But in the end there is no substitute for truth, especially when delivering bad news.

Leaders avoid speaking in anger. Project teams have tense moments. Passionate debate can become angry and ugly with the turn of a phrase. If this happens, lower the temperature by focusing on objective facts and don't make it personal. Try a little humor. Add some perspective. After conflict bring the parties together to help heal the wounds. The team needs leadership to keep things on an even keel and to keep grudges from forming.

Finally, be clear and be brief.

Quick Ref

1. Interpersonal Communications
- Pick the right mode
- Listen first and well
- Use tact but tell the truth
- Remember the golden rule
- Don't speak in anger
- Keep the temperature down and the perspective objective
- Try some humor
- No grudges; try to heal wounds
- Time communications properly
- Choose the audience wisely
- Be clear and brief

Structured Planning/Organizing

Planning - Building the Plan

In the first section, we discussed "knowing the plan" as a basic plank. The PM works with the team to build a simple plan. Simpler generally means easier to grasp and to fix when disrupted. The plan is rooted in the project objective(s). What is the goal? What does success look like? The PM must articulate the desired end-state to the team once it is confirmed with the project sponsor and customers.

The plan-building exercise delivers the first-cut project schedule: basically a list of tasks to be performed, by when, by whom, at what cost, and with what dependencies. This includes the critical and often tricky 'task estimating' skill. Team members usually tend to either over or underestimate the time required to accomplish a specific task; the more seasoned the performer, generally the better the estimate. Credibility is at stake with task estimates and associated ability to hit overall deadlines, so PM Leaders work closely with performers on 'time budgets.' PMs also build a contingency buffer within the plan. Scheduling tools like MSP are often used because they allow visual representations of the plan as well as dependent task linkage. High-end project planning tools like MSP can be convenient, helpful and sometimes crucial to success. Just as often plans can be effectively managed on spreadsheets. Whatever management software is available, PMs should avoid unnecessary complexity.

Once steps and dependencies are understood at the right level of detail (enough so that everyone knows what tasks they own, the associated time budgets, due dates and dependencies), the leader explicitly secures commitment from all resources for the sake of clarity. In the best case this happens face to face, either in a team setting or individually. The same dynamics apply when articulating explicit roles and responsibilities. On most teams there is duty/responsibility overlap so it's crucial that everyone understand where boundaries lie. Team morale tends to be better when everyone focuses on his own job until and unless asked for help.

Organizing - Meeting Management

The PM establishes meeting cadence by communicating recurring meeting schedules and setting expectations for how ad-hoc meetings will be handled. Typically regular meetings are held on some combination of daily, weekly, and monthly cadence. Many factors drive meeting cadence and the PM is responsible for pulling them together to best effect. Meetings are critically important to the project, and managing them is a key PM skill. This is discussed further in the next "PM Skills" section.

Organizing - Issue Management

The trick to successful issue management is having a process for getting the problem to the right person for timely resolution. The PM helps identify issues but mainly acts as referee and scorekeeper by ensuring they are properly catalogued, documented and routed for action and resolution. A regular forum for issue discussion may be necessary, or the PM may manage issues "offline" via calls/email.

Organizing - Scope Management

Scope change management is crucial since scope changes can severely endanger effective project delivery. Scope management boils down to the project sponsor being in place and empowered to make timely tradeoff decisions. The PM ensures proposed changes are assessed, presented to the sponsor for decision, and acted on.

*Quick Ref **

2. Structured Planning/Organizing
- Simpler is generally better
- Define the end state first
- Identify steps to end state
- Identify dependencies
- Identify risks/alternatives
- Identify skill sets
- Identify task owners
- Identify roles and responsibilities overall
- Identify target dates
- Secure commitment
- Set project meeting/communications cadence
- Define scope change management process
- Define escalation path/process

Meeting Management

PMs are often judged by how they run meetings. A good rule of thumb is to keep meetings as focused as possible, as brief as possible, and involve as few people as necessary. As the leader, the PM has the opportunity to waste many people's time on a recurring basis. Even if the leader doesn't do anything else particularly well, the team will greatly appreciate strong meeting management.

A good first step is recognizing that meetings are generally a necessary evil and should be minimized. That said, projects would fail without them. This is because the direct information exchange meetings provide is key to close and continued coordination among many parties. But this only works when there is focus on the meeting agenda and not a free-for-all "gabfest." The more people in the meeting, the harder it is to maintain focus. This is where strong meeting management skills come in.

At the start of a project, the PM should consider a brainstorming session with the core team to discuss the overall need for meetings. A list of meetings by type, purpose, owner, recurrence and attendees will emerge. This list forms the basis of the master meeting schedule, which the PM tweaks as necessary. Of course, some ad-hoc meetings will be required too, and the same meeting management skills apply to those.

The concept of a meeting owner is also important. If I own the meeting, I'm responsible for running it. Hijacking meetings by taking them in directions not intended is both aggravating and non-productive for everyone. The meeting owner/leader must politely, but firmly, protect his meeting turf or risk participants becoming disinterested and losing focus.

The basic idea for meeting conduct is to identify who is present, articulate an agenda, navigate the agenda with little straying, close the meeting with a brief summary, allow an opportunity for questions/comments, and then send out brief notes documenting the summary. At times more detailed notes may be required but generally a summary suffices. The meeting owner can easily accomplish this with a little practice and confidence. Many meetings require use of conference call bridges and associated web-cast tools since work teams are often geographically dispersed. It's not uncommon to be swapping emails and texts with meeting members while running a webcast of meeting content over a live conference call line!

Most meetings can easily be kept to between 15-45 minutes if the leader sticks to the agenda and keeps things moving. Teams learn to cooperate particularly when the leader calls them on wandering off subject too much. This can be done in a friendly way with humor, and everyone appreciates the time returned to them from a meeting completed early.

***Quick Ref ***

3. Meeting Management
- Have a clear agenda
- Keep meetings focused and brief
- Acknowledge a meeting "hijacker," then steer him back on course
- Use a consistent simple format
- Provide agenda/notes to all attendees
- Defer complex issues offline
- Have a sense of humor

Time and Task Management

It's often said that PMs have to "herd the cats." That is, lead, manage, and cajole team members toward mission accomplishment. So they have to be available and attentive. In order to achieve this state of readiness, the PM must have full command of his time.

Having full command of one's time means being highly organized such that there is little to no wasted time overall. This means knowing appropriate PM roles/tasks and not casually straying from them. It means delegating and holding others accountable as well as oneself. It means working on the right things in the right order. It means having the discipline to accept that there may not be any immediate tasks in the queue without manufacturing some or doing someone else's job.

The PM who commands his time is available to react promptly to any number of important unplanned demands on his time. This can be solving problems, making additional communications outside the normal channels, or even taking on other efforts that would not interfere with the primary mission and may be tangentially helpful.

**Quick Ref **

4. Time and Task Management
- Plan the use of time
- Guard your time closely
- More available time = quicker response
- Don't spend time on others' jobs

Communications Management

The PM will create and maintain a communications plan. This can be a simple matrix of when, how, between whom, by what means and on what frequency ongoing team communications will occur. For example, there will be regular team meetings, executive or senior management reviews, status reports, and implementation planning messaging to name a few types.

The communication management effort keeps interested parties abreast of project status, at the appropriate level of detail, on an ongoing basis. With a standing agreement that all is considered on-track unless otherwise indicated in planned communications, stakeholders can stay plugged in with very little time and effort. This approach also minimizes the need for management interruption of the work effort and aims to keep all communications as brief and clear as possible.

**Quick Ref **

5. Communications Management
- Good communications are a PM priority
- Poorly managed communications hurt the mission
- Ensure all know status at all times

- Maintain flexible communications recipient lists
- Modify communications plan as required
- All communications must be as brief and clear as possible

Accountability

As a rule everything that happens on the project is the PM Leader's responsibility. "Responsible" in this case also means accountable, regardless of the "root cause." The project team will respect the PM's willingness and ability to take the heat, even as he holds teammates accountable in the background. This is especially true if the leader doesn't resort to a zero defect mentality the first time something goes wrong. Commonly shared adversity builds strong team bonds.

Quick Ref

6. Accountability
- The buck stops with you
- Delegate authority but retain responsibility
- No zero defect mentality
- Inspires loyalty and good will
- Demonstrates competency and responsibility
- Hold others accountable as appropriate

Handling Bad News

Leaders must know bad news quickly. The reason is simple: bad news usually involves problems, and problems can't be fixed until they are acknowledged and understood. So the quicker they are addressed, the quicker they can be fixed. Also, the longer the problem exists, generally the greater the loss to the project/mission. A big problem manifested early and remedied quickly may have minimal impact overall. But even a relatively small problem left un-addressed for long can be catastrophic.

Finally, it's important for the team to see the leader as calm and resolved under pressure, not overly nervous, afraid or lacking poise. A good leader knows he's not perfect and willingly admits when he's wrong.

Quick Ref

7. Accept/Deliver Bad News
- Seek bad news; accept calmly
- Leads to fixes/improvements
- Deliver bad news timely/calmly
- Don't shoot the messenger
- Pros thrive when things go wrong
- Admitting mistakes shows strength; set the example
- Keep a sense of perspective and humor

Rewarding Success

There are many ways to reward success. Some are official and enumerated in an organization's human resources policies/procedures. Others are more personal and intangible. Effective leaders know their team members. They pay close attention to personality nuances so they know how best to reward success. People generally work harder, longer, better and are happier when they know they are appreciated.

Examples of rewards include: a private personal thanks from the leader, informal recognition by the leader in front of the team or wider organizational audience, formal recognition by the organization (possibly including financial or other tangible award/compensation), or input to the formal performance review process. The people are by far the most important asset to the team so treat them as such.

**Quick Ref **

8. Rewarding Success
- Unique to the personality
- Public vs. private consideration
- Key driver for job satisfaction
- Be consistent and equitable

- Know your team members
- Team members are the most important resource

Coaching and Mentoring

The PM Leader need not be the grizzled sage in order to coach and mentor team members. First off, the PM is the leader because he knows how to lead, plan, organize, motivate and execute. In a way, the leader coaches everyone by setting the example. By organizing the project, keeping it on track, resolving issues, heading off trouble, thinking ahead, and looking out for the team and the mission in general, the PM sets a huge (hopefully good) example for the team to see.

Team members may express specific interest in understanding the PM role. The leader should respond with interest and enthusiasm to such inquiries/interest to the extent possible and appropriate. Doing so shows the leader's interest in the team as individuals past the immediate project. It's an honor to have the chance to coach/mentor; leaders look to make the most of such opportunities.

**Quick Ref **

9. Coaching and Mentoring
- Your role sets examples, good and bad
- Respond to coaching interest with

enthusiasm
- Provide timely/consistent/useful information to interested parties
- Demonstrate overall concern for teammates
- Remember the help you got along the way

Handling Change

No project plan survives without change. PMs must build the most flexible plan possible with the expectation it will change. This means a built-in, robust process for managing the inevitable changes.

The team's mindset is also crucial to effectively handling modifications to the plan. Some change should be expected and viewed as a necessary adjustment to evolving circumstances. The team and sponsors expect the leader to find the way forward through strife and uncertainty. PMs lead the process of deciding whether or not proposed changes are worth the cost in time, budget, re-work, and frustration. Then they work with key stakeholders to drive, communicate, and implement decisions. Finally, leaders bookmark these plan changes for future "Lessons Learned" session reference.

Quick Ref

10. Handling Change
- No project plan survives without change
- Embrace change; have a process for managing it
- Remain calm with sense of urgency in the face of unexpected change

- Note change drivers for possible "Lessons Learned" relevance

Motivating the Team

Teams work better when they have high morale. Leaders know this and work hard to motivate the team. Along these lines, here are some "Do's:"

- Show a positive attitude
- Remain cool, especially when under pressure
- Show resolve
- Seek input
- Make timely decisions
- Take responsibility
- Admit mistakes
- Help with the hard work
- Provide morale support
- Show a sense of humor
- Be firm, but fair
- Show empathy
- Be loyal
- Be courageous
- Use good judgment
- Show commitment to the mission and team
- Never quit

These "motivators" manifest in many ways, large and small, throughout a project. They may make the difference in your team's success or failure when the going gets tough.

**Quick Ref **

11. Motivating the Team
- High morale equals better outcomes
- Show a positive attitude
- Remain cool especially when under pressure
- Show resolve
- Seek input
- Make timely decisions
- Take responsibility
- Admit mistakes
- Help with the hard work
- Provide morale support
- Show a sense of humor
- Be firm, but fair
- Show empathy
- Be loyal
- Be courageous
- Be committed to the mission and team
- Use good judgment
- Never quit

Project Accounting

A PM can get into hot water quickly for failing to account for project budget. Obviously it's important that the PM control expenditures on the project, but usually there are other parties involved to guide/assist. Depending on the organization and project type, the complexity of this task is highly variable.

Let's look at the fundamental factors involved. First, what is the project spending money on? People mainly, but often material too. How much money (aka "budget") do we have for each of these categories? Do these expenditures need to happen on specific timelines? Is the project required to publish spending forecasts? Capture actual spending? Compare the two and show a variance? Put this information into a particular tool/system?

If finance professionals are involved they will know the "accounting requirements." If you can work with spreadsheets, you can keep track of all the basic information on most projects. For example, a typical spreadsheet may have the weeks of the project on one axis and the names of the team on the other. Each cell may have the expected (projected) work hours. The spreadsheet sums these hours by person/week, along with associated totals for the weeks and the project. A similar sheet can be made with actuals in place of the projected numbers. With this information the PM can easily calculate the total "spend" compared to the projected "spend" and show the "burn rate" along the way. This type of tracking can also be done for equipment purchases and represents conceptually how the PM can keep an eye on the project budget with very simple tools. If more complex work is required (and it will be for many types of projects), the PM can seek assistance from accounting or finance personnel.

Often the more difficult part of budget management is ensuring the team understands what is expected, and then following through to maintain forecast accuracy. This can be tough because it won't always be easy for team members to anticipate work hours with great precision. This is especially true if they are only partially assigned to the project and have several other work obligations throughout the life of the project.

A good rule of thumb is to gain an understanding of the project budget-tracking requirement from finance/management, and then meet with the team to devise a capture and reporting mechanism that meets requirements. This will allow the PM to report accurately and timely, highlighting any unplanned variances for sponsor awareness and/or assistance.

**Quick Ref **

12. Project Accounting
- Not difficult, but make sure the requirement is understood
- Get "level-of-effort" commitment from all performers
- Capture estimates
- Capture actuals
- Encourage proactive adjustments
- Hold team performers accountable
- Report accounting status promptly and consistently
- Seek assistance/guidance from sponsors and finance group as required

Risk and Issue Management

Risk and Issue management is pretty straightforward and should be kept simple. This is because risk-management on the project level has become a cottage industry to the point that many PMs lose sight of the purpose while trying to keep up with the many techniques, tools and methodologies.

The PM leads the team in identifying possible barriers to project success, both proactively and as they arise. Some are *potential* occurrences, deficiencies, or negative circumstances (**risks**) and some are situations *already* causing problems (**issues**). The leader works with the team to assess the nature, scope, likelihood, and severity of potential risks. He then makes plans to counter, accept or simply "watch" them.

The PM identifies and then takes positive action to resolve issues. There are many ways to categorize risks and issues in terms of severity: Red-Yellow-Green, High-Medium-Low, A-B-C, etc. What's important is that the PM manages both risks and issues, and to the degree possible avoids surprising the project sponsor with problems that should and could have been foreseen, prevented and/or avoided.

Quick Ref

13. Risk and Issue Management
- Don't over-complicate the risk/issue management process
- Assess the nature, scope, likelihood, and severity of potential risks
- Make plans to counter, accept or simply "watch" the risks
- Identify issues and take positive action to resolve them
- Use a simple, rational model to measure, track (e.g., Red-Yellow-Green)
- Ensure sponsors understand both risks and issues
- Use team to help identify and categorize
- Report status of both as a part of recurring reporting
- Be on the lookout for risks and issues constantly
- Review risks and issues with the team on a regular basis

Status Reporting

Status reporting, like risk and issue management, can be done in many formats and via many specific approaches. The project sponsor or other responsible project champion will usually set at least some high level reporting requirements. The PM should be proactive in suggesting formats and assisting the sponsor and team in arriving at a "right-sized" status reporting process.

Ideally project status reporting is done against a baseline plan with the focus on how the team is progressing against plan milestone tasks. Report on a regular cadence; weekly is typical, perhaps with a quarterly update to senior management on longer project efforts. Often key accomplishments are communicated along with next milestones to be tackled, and specific risks and/or issues are called out. Management should be able to glean essential status from the report very quickly (seconds).

Usually the PM will assign a quick-reference indicator of project health in the status report (use of Red, Yellow, Green is typical) in order to save readers time. Green might get little attention, yellow will raise some eyebrows, and red will have sponsors reading the details. Remember, it's the PM's job to get the project rolling and keep it on track through successful mission accomplishment. If that means pulling in sponsors for external assistance, the status report is a good place to document those needs. Not to say the PM could/should wait until the latest status to surface issues, but they should definitely be documented there. In short, the status report is the PM's key tool to document progress and the need for assistance when necessary. It is both a crucial project artifact and an important communication tool. Keep it as simple, brief and easily used as possible.

Quick Ref

14. Status Reporting
- Use a simple, brief, clear format
- Report progress vs. plan
- Report issues and need for help
- Document risks
- Be consistent and timely in reporting

Personal Organization & Time Management

Personal organization and time management are bread and butter skills for the PM Leader. If the leader can't work to his own correct priorities he will never be able to keep the team focused on correct plan priorities. The better he manages his time, the more of it he has available to accomplish planned tasks and to successfully react to unplanned tasks. Since the PM is essentially the quarterback of the project team, he must be available to respond to project needs quickly. As the focal point of many if not most project coordination activities, he cannot afford to fall behind in personal communications like email and phone messages. Doing so invites unpleasant surprises.

For these reasons the PM must take steps to keep his "slate" clear as much of the time as possible. First and foremost, this means his taking on only appropriate roles and responsibilities and that all team members follow suit. Next, the PM stays on top of inbound email/phone messages and does not allow them to accumulate unread. In doing so the leader is able to perform ongoing triage of actions, and work on the most important items in the correct order given the overall situation and mission. This can be tricky business and takes practice and discipline to master (read Stephen Covey's *The 7 Habits of Highly Effective People* for more on this). Addressing the "squeaky wheels" first is often not the right answer but can be difficult to resist. By remaining aware, available, and vigilant, the PM is the guardian of project scope and the team's focus on completing it on time and within budget.

A quick word about email: remember it is easily misread/misunderstood.

When communicating by email, be professional, courteous and neutral in tone when dealing with people you don't know well. If you are angry, proceed with caution. Remember, email is captured in black and white and is practically irretrievable.

**Quick Ref **

15. Personal Organization and Time/Email Management

- Bread and butter skills for the PM Leader
- PM is the quarterback and must be responsive to enable problem solving
- To be responsive, the PM must be organized and use time wisely
- Prioritize and work to the right priorities;

do not get habitually behind
- Ensure the team is working to the right priorities per the plan
- Delegate as necessary to create additional time when pressed
- Establish "To:" and "CC:" rules for email; minimize the number coming in
- Create an archive to allow quick storage and retrieval of key emails
- Store important emails, not all emails
- Store "pending work" emails or otherwise use a "reminder" technique
- Respond promptly to emails
- Be courteous and brief in email traffic
- Use lots of white space on email content
- Do not respond emotionally on email; it is easy to be misunderstood
- When you **must** be understood, meet face to face
- Avoid using email to circumvent organizational boundaries (i.e. don't go around or over someone you should not bypass just because you can easily do so in email)

Resolving Conflict

PM leaders are positioned to identify conflict and resolve it. They face it squarely and objectively. Get the facts and remain as unemotional as possible. When leaders get emotional anyway (passion is a good thing when controlled), they remember to keep things from becoming personal.

There are volumes on the subject of conflict resolution far beyond the scope of this manual. However, a forthright approach to putting issues/conflicts on the table in a safe environment where discussions and even arguments can proceed without retribution or hard feelings usually works. Such an environment will not happen by accident. The PM Leader must foster it. Actions may include taking conflict "off-line" to a smaller setting when it arises in too large a group to be dealt with, preferably face-to-face. Healthy families argue, fight and make up. The project team can and should as well. Remember to team-build along the way to avoid preventable conflict, and make recovery from strife easier.

Quick Ref

16. Resolving Conflict
- Face the music
- Be tactful and forthright
- Aim for compromise and harmony
- Take what you can get
- Don't make it personal and don't hold grudges
- Remember to proactively team-build
- Encourage the larger view and add a little humor when it works

Personality Types

Leaders get to know the various personality traits and types. They can do this by reading on the subject and taking a personality inventory. A couple of leading versions are "Personalysis" and the "Myers-Briggs Personality Inventory." These and similar tools help illustrate personality preferences and tendencies. Are you more introverted or extroverted? A relative "thinker" or a "feeler?" How do you tend to behave under stress that might be different from when everything is normal? This information can not only help leaders understand behavioral tendencies, it can also reveal why they react to, and work with some personality types better than others. Such insights empower leaders to work better with the full range of personalities likely to be found among their teammates.

Quick Ref

17. Personality Types
- Personalysis; Myers-Briggs, etc.
- There are a number of distinctive personality traits people have
- Not all traits blend well together naturally
- Understanding personality traits and profiles drives coping strategy
- Know yourself and your own traits

- Identify your teammates' traits
- Find ways to work better together given the enhanced understanding

PM Leader as an "Outsider"

Often PMs are contract workers. Just as often they are full-time, but are seated organizationally in a pool of project management professionals who serve the organization as a common resource. In either case, they usually find themselves outside the normal "line" business or IT organizational structure.

Project team resources are sometimes shared between project and other "line" duties. It is a natural leadership tendency for the PM to look out for team members on or off the project. This can bring the PM into contention with line management over the use of project resources. It's important in such cases that the PM use the normal issue escalation chain to get resolution, and not directly engage line management unless there is an established positive working relationship. This is because the PM often has little power outside the project structure. The project sponsor though, by definition should have the scope of control to successfully and rapidly resolve any conflicts that may arise.

**Quick Ref **

18. PM Leader as an "Outsider"
- The Leader must remember that at times he is an "outsider"
- PMs are often not full time employees or in the "line" management chain
- Shared project resources may also report to "line" management
- Understand explicit and implied organizational roles of others
- Use the issue escalation chain and the project champion to resolve shared resource issues

Ed Daniel

Conclusion

A PM Leader with a good plan, leading a competent team, supported by a determined sponsor is a key ingredient to project success.

Anyone with enough desire can master the PM Leader discipline. This handbook stands as a ready reference to practical skills and principles the PM Leader will need along the way.

All the best.

Ed Daniel

<u>Appendices</u>

Related PM Leader Information.

Appendix A: Common PM Leader Pitfalls

- Trusting too fully, too quickly

- Failing to take charge in a firm and approachable way

- Failing to clarify roles and responsibilities well enough

- Allowing meetings to be hijacked

- Allowing meetings to remain unfocused and last too long

- Allowing project customers to make changes outside a well-defined, controlled process

- Failing to adequately control own email communications

- Failing to be organized and responsive enough in general

- Failing to delegate properly, and then being overwhelmed with detail work that should have been delegated

- Capturing meeting notes at the wrong level of detail (usually too much), missing key points and the gist of the meeting

- Over-supervising and alienating otherwise competent team members

- Becoming too involved in line management issues

- Thinking they have to be either the "hard-guy" or the "clown" – neither extreme is appropriate

- Failing to be themselves and not realizing you can't fake a different personality for long

- Failing to stand up for team members at the appropriate time

- Failing to hold team members accountable

- Not reporting bad news quickly enough

- Allowing the team to become overcommitted

Appendix B: PM Role-Play Scenarios

- Respond to a new work request (scope increase)

- Deflect a meeting hijack attempt

- Lead a rollout call where issues are mounting

- Lead a lessons learned session

- Write a lessons learned document

- Lead a requirements gathering session ('analyst' task - good insight)

- Develop functional requirements ('analyst' task - good insight)

- Plan a weekly team meeting

- Lead a weekly team meeting

- Draft an initial work plan via collaborative meeting

- Lead a roles & responsibilities identification session

- Provide status to a group of sponsors

- Create a project cost tracking spreadsheet

- Lead a technical "deep dive" session as facilitator

- Counsel a team member (remedial and/or positive feedback)

- Counsel a team member (personal / professional issues)

About the Author

Ed Daniel is an experienced leader and manager. His experience includes a variety of field and staff leadership roles in the USMC, at both junior and senior levels, within combat arms and in various support functions, deployed and within the US.

In addition to his military experience, the author has served in a variety of Project and Program Manager positions in the commercial sector as well as on US government engagements. This work has required leadership in a number of austere circumstances, locations and roles.

In a concurrent career thread, Mr. Daniel has spent over fifteen years in the business and information technology consulting industry. This work began with Andersen Consulting for several years and continued with the launch and operation of a small consultancy providing similar services on a boutique scale.

Throughout Mr. Daniel's career the common theme has been successful mission accomplishment through dynamic leadership, management and project management. He has had the privilege of leading numerous business and information technology project teams, in a variety of industries, through successful project and program delivery. The key principles, skills, and techniques the author presents in this handbook are for him the essential common ingredients for success.

About the Logo

The black table against the grey background represents the "round table," egalitarian approach to teamwork, with the team members represented by the blue circles and the PM Leader by the red.

The commonly drawn swords represent unified commitment. The ship represents a shared journey leading to mission accomplishment and achievement.

www.ingramcontent.com/pod-product-compliance
Lightning Source LLC
Chambersburg PA
CBHW061516180526
45171CB00001B/209